# The Adventures of Young Ambedkar

## A Note on the Author

A medical doctor by training, Devyani Khobragade joined the Indian Foreign Service in 1999. She is currently Joint Secretary in the Ministry of External Affairs. This is her first children's book.

# The Adventures of Young Ambedkar

Devyani Khobragade

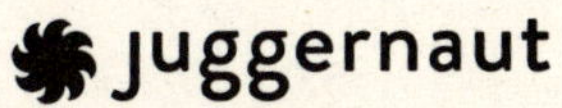

JUGGERNAUT BOOKS
C-I-128, First Floor, Sangam Vihar, Near Holi Chowk,
New Delhi 110080, India

First published by Juggernaut Books 2020



10 9 8 7 6 5 4 3 2

P-ISBN: 9789353450809
E-ISBN: 9789353450816



Typeset in Adobe Caslon Pro by R. Ajith Kumar, Noida

Printed and bound in India by Replika Press Pvt. Ltd.

# Author's Note

I wrote this book to educate my daughters about the struggles of the Dalit community. To capture their imagination, I came up with a children's story about Dr B.R. Ambedkar as a little boy, staying true to the context but adding some fictional elements. And it worked! My children read it and were curious to know more. They even gave me editorial feedback such as 'who says stuff like "he was a roly-poly child"!' And Shaira offered to draw some pictures for the book, like the one on the next page.

Thanks to Chiki Sarkar of Juggernaut for publishing this book, and to my dear daughters, Amaya and Shaira, and my niece Sitara for inspiring me to write it.

Shaira

# 1

More than a hundred years ago, India was ruled by the British, who came from faraway England. The British Indian empire was very large. It stretched from Burma (now called Myanmar) in the east to Afghanistan in the west, and Kashmir and the Himalayas in the north to Ceylon (now Sri Lanka) in the south. Almost bang in the middle of this vast empire was a small, sleepy town called Mhow.

The British had a large army there. Soldiers from many parts of India were stationed there. They lived in barracks and their children went to the army school. At the time of our story the headmaster of this school was an army man named Ramji Sakpal.

Ramji had joined the British army, like his father.

He was not born in Mhow. His village was far away, near the sea. It was called Ambavadi – after its many mango orchards. As a child, Ramji had played hide-and-seek in the orchards. He and his friends had climbed the trees, plucked mangoes and sometimes thrown them at each other.

As a young boy, Ramji was married off to a girl named Bhimabai. Ramji's job took them to many places and they had many children, most of whom died due to various illnesses. On 14 April 1891, when they were living in Mhow, Bhimabai gave birth to their fourteenth child – a boy, who was named Bhimrao after his mother.

Ramji and Bhimabai were very happy to have a healthy child. This newborn had round, fat cheeks, large, dark eyes and a head full of black curls.

When Bhim was three, Ramji retired from the army as a headmaster with the rank of subedar. This was the highest rank an Indian could reach in the British army in those days. The family moved from Mhow to Satara, a pretty little town in the hills of Maharashtra.

The Sakpals were a large family. One of Bhim's

sisters had died, and her children lived with Ramji and Bhimabai. They lived in a pucca house with a veranda and a sloping tiled roof. Bhim's elder siblings played in the veranda and among the trees surrounding the house. Every now and then, Bhim would climb on to one of the large windows to catch a glimpse of them and ask if he could join them. They would run into the house and carry Bhim in their arms and let him play alongside for a bit.

Sadly, when Bhim was about five years old, his mother passed away. And Bhim's aunt moved to Satara to look after the children in the Sakpal household.

# 2

As a child, Bhim was especially curious about the books the older children read. He often picked them up to see what was in there, but he could not make sense of it.

So when his father told him that he would soon be joining school, Bhim was excited. He would finally learn to read those mysterious books! Bhim knew he would have to walk a long distance every day to get to the school, but this did not put him off.

On the first day, when Bhim and his father entered the school, the bald and grumpy principal told Ramji, 'You should thank the British for allowing low-caste children to study in school along with high-caste children.'

Bhim knew he belonged to the Mahar caste. People said it was a low caste, but he didn't understand what it meant.

Bhim walked into the classroom, where he saw a group of children his age. Just as he was about to sit with them, a thundering voice stopped him.

'Hey you! Sit there, in that corner. You can't sit next to them.' It was the class attendant, an old man with a big belly. 'And from tomorrow onward bring your own gunny mat to class every day and take it back home with you. I don't want to be polluted by your mat while cleaning the room.'

Young Bhim was confused. He wasn't allowed to sit with his classmates, whose mats were spread across the room. He did not understand why he was being separated from the others in class. He felt sad and scared. School wasn't as much fun as he had imagined it would be. He decided to ask his father why people at school avoided his touch.

But that evening, Ramji was busy preparing to leave town on some work. So Bhim could not ask him the question that had been niggling at his mind all day.

2x8=16

# 3

Next day at school, Bhim was quiet and careful.

During the break, he hesitated to join the kids who had run out of the room to play kho-kho. But they knew Bhim could run fast and each team was keen to take him. Bhim had a good time playing with his classmates.

At the end of the break, they were all tired and thirsty. They ran to the earthen water pitchers to get a drink of water.

Bhim waited for his turn. Before he could pour himself some water from the pitcher, the class attendant came running and pushed Bhim aside.

'Stay away! If you touch that, nobody will drink from it. Everyone will have to go thirsty.'

From then on, whenever Bhim needed water, he had to request the class attendant. The old man made sure that Bhim did not touch the pitcher when he poured water into his little palms.

One hot summer day, the attendant was busy elsewhere. And no one else would give Bhim water from the earthen pitchers. Poor Bhim remained thirsty the whole day.

He was impatient and could not wait any more for his father to return. He decided to ask his aunt or elder sister why the people in his school would not touch him.

# 4

However, before Bhim could talk to his aunt, something troubling happened.

Bhim had thick, curly hair. Most children in his class applied oil on their hair and combed it back so neatly that it appeared pasted on to their head. But Bhim's hair was long and his loose curls looked untidy.

One day, his teacher scolded him. 'How long has it been since you went to a barber?' he asked, pointing at Bhim's hair.

Bhim paused before answering, 'Never . . .'

'What do you mean? Who cuts your hair?' The teacher was irritated.

'My elder sister or aunt,' Bhim said sheepishly.

Bhim knew that the other kids went to the barber for a haircut. But he and his brothers had their hair cut by their aunt or elder sister at home. In fact, his aunt and sister were quite expert barbers!

'Oh yes, of course. You are a Mahar,' the teacher said. 'Go get a haircut today. Don't show up in school again with such long hair.'

That evening, Bhim asked his aunt, 'Why don't we go to the barber for our haircut, Aayta? Don't we have enough money?'

'No, we have money, but no barber will cut the hair of people from the Mahar or any other untouchable caste,' she answered.

'What is caste?' Bhim asked.

His aunt did not know how to answer this simple question.

She began hesitantly. 'Well, you see, in your school, there's a principal and there are teachers. Their forefathers did the same job. And the temple on the way to your school – the priests there are priests because their ancestors were also priests.'

Bhim used to look curiously at the temple every time he walked past it. He wanted to know more about the idol inside and all the rituals around it that he had heard of but never seen. But his father had softly held him back, telling him that they couldn't go inside.

His aunt continued, 'And the sweepers who clean your school and the roads, they are doing the work their forefathers did. And their children will continue to do the same because they belong to the caste that is supposed to do that particular work.'

'Is that why they are regarded dirty and low?'

'Yes, pora.'

'But we don't clean the streets. Why do the teachers and class assistant avoid my touch?'

'That is because our forefathers used to clean the streets. That was the only work they were allowed to do.'

'How come Baba did not clean streets but worked as a teacher in the army?' he asked.

His aunt smiled. 'Bhau and our Baba went to school and college. The British allowed even the low castes to study. That is why they could take up other jobs. But they are still considered untouchables, Bhim.' She tried to explain, 'High-caste people do not touch us or anything touched by us. Untouchables have to live away from high-caste people.'

Bhim had more questions.

'But Aatya, why should it be so? Are we really dirty?' Bhim asked, angry and helpless.

'Nahi, pora.' His aunt pulled him into a soft hug. 'On the other hand, many untouchable castes clear our streets and homes of garbage and dead animals and keep them clean.'

She then tried to cheer him up by turning his attention to something else. 'Run along now and cook some rice and mutton with your brothers, will you? I'm tired today. You boys should look after yourselves.'

Bhim loved cooking mutton pulao with his brothers. All they had to do was throw some rice, mutton, spices, salt and water into a pan and bring it to a boil. But that day, he was sad. He wondered if he should ask his teacher, Ambedkar Saheb, to let him sit with his classmates.

# 5

Bhim hated getting up early in the morning, especially in winter, when it was cold and damp. But Bhim's father woke his children up at the crack of dawn to sing devotional songs called abhangs with him. He was strict like a teacher and Bhim did not like it.

His father would tell Bhim, 'Even the rooster gets up early to crow every morning. Why can't you?'

'Because I am not a rooster,' a sleepy Bhim would retort.

'That's why I'm not asking you to crow, but to sing an abhang instead,' Ramji would say with a chuckle.

Abhangs are Marathi and Hindi songs written

by bhakti saints four to five hundred years ago and they are sung to this day. The abhang that Ramji sang most often was one by Sant Tukaram, the saint-poet loved by all Marathi speakers. It goes, *mungi ani rao, amha sarkhachi jeev*, which means 'the smallest ant and the king, to me they are all equal'.

As he grew older, Bhim started understanding the abhangs. He especially liked the ones written by the saints Namdev and Kabir, and he continued to listen to them even as a grown-up.

One day, Ambedkar Saheb spoke to his class about the life and works of these devotional saints. After the class, Bhim walked up to the teacher and said, 'Sir, if everyone is equal, as the saints said they are, then I should be allowed to sit with my classmates.'

The teacher, who had always admired Bhim's courage, said, 'Yes, you are right, Bhim. But if you sit with the other kids, many high-caste people will stop sending their children to the school and we will have to close it.'

Ambedkar Saheb couldn't change the rules of the school, but he wanted to help Bhim in some way. 'I see that you want to change things that are unfair. I believe you will do it. I will change your surname in the school records from Sakpal to mine – Ambedkar. This way you will not be shunned and you will also remember my words and work to bring about change.'

From then on Bhimrao Sakpal was known as Bhimrao Ramji Ambedkar.

# 6

Despite the change in name, things did not improve for Bhim.

The higher-caste kids went to each other's homes during festivals and weddings. But Bhim could not visit their houses nor would they come to his. When they talked about such gatherings at school, Bhim listened to their stories feeling left out and friendless.

At home too, Bhim was unhappy. His siblings blamed him for their mother's death as she had been sickly since Bhim's birth. Ramji had remarried as he needed help to raise the kids. But Bhim didn't like seeing another woman take his mother's place. To make matters worse, his father pushed him hard to study. But Ramji knew that Bhim was a good student and had great plans for his son. That is why he made Bhim work hard.

One day, Bhim heard his father speak about Bombay, a big city, where people from all castes and many places lived alongside each other. Thinking it would be a good place for him, Bhim decided to run away without telling anyone.

He knew he would need money to go to Bombay. He stealthily searched his aunt's purse. But there was very little money in it. Somehow this filled Bhim with shame. He recalled what his aunt had said about education giving low-caste people a chance to better their lot. He decided to do what his father had always wanted and to take his studies seriously from then on.

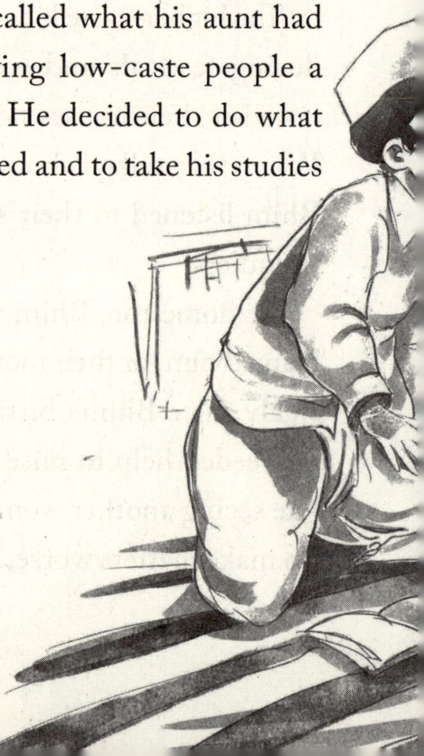

# 7

When Bhim was about nine years old, his father and stepmother moved to another town called Koregaon. Ramji was now working as a cashier for a project run by the British to build a water reservoir in Koregaon. There was a famine in the region and the project was started to provide employment to the poor there, who were dying of hunger. Bhim and the other kids, however, continued to live in Satara with their aunt.

Ramji wanted his sons to join him in Koregaon during their summer vacations. The boys were excited at the thought of the journey by train. They started preparing for their holiday a few days ahead. New clothes were bought – English shirts of soft muslin and dhotis with gold borders. They also got themselves new caps and shoes. On top of that, their aunt gave each of them some pocket money to spend on the train.

And then came the big day of travel. Their aunt cried as she put them on the train. 'I will miss you a lot,' she said. She reminded them for the umpteenth time, 'Be careful on the train and don't get down anywhere before Masur station.'

Once on the train, they promptly bought lemon sodas with their pocket money. It was thrilling. Hours went by quickly, like the wayside trees that rushed past the window.

When they got off at Masur, they parked themselves prominently on the railway platform so that their father or his assistant could spot them easily. An hour passed but no one turned up.

'Didn't you inform Baba when we would be reaching?' Bhim asked his brother.

'Yes, yes! I wrote him a letter saying we would be arriving today on this train,' said his brother, reassuringly.

Their excitement soon turned into worry.

The stationmaster, who had been watching the boys, approached them and asked what the matter was.

The boys explained the situation to him.

'You look like you are from a decent family. Are you Deshmukhs or Chavans?' The stationmaster thought the boys were from a high caste.

'We are Mahars,' Bhim blurted out.

Instantly the stationmaster's face and manner changed. The kindness and concern disappeared, and he stomped away disgusted. Soon, the drivers of all the bullock carts and horse carts parked outside the railway station had learned that the kids were untouchables. None of them was ready to take the boys to Koregaon.

The stationmaster did not want any trouble with these kids at his station. When it became quite dark, he asked the boys, 'Can one of you drive a bullock cart?' 'Yes, we

can,' they answered, finally feeling a little hopeful.

'Okay, then. Give this man double the fare and you can sit in his cart and ride it, while he walks along.'

The bullock cart owner did not want to sit with the untouchable boys for fear of getting polluted by their touch. But he couldn't resist the money the same untouchable boys were ready to pay.

The boys rode for a long time. As they approached a dry riverbed, the owner asked them to stop the cart and said, 'You boys better eat now. You won't get any water to drink with your food after we cross this river.'

The cart owner then vanished to a nearby village for his meal. Bhim and his party opened their tiffin. One of them went to the river to fetch some water, but came back without any.

'There's nothing but puddles of stinky water full of cow dung!' he told the rest. 'Oh, then we can't even eat!' exclaimed Bhim, who was by now very hungry and tired.

They resumed the journey when the cart owner returned. It was around nine at night and the road was deserted. Suddenly, the man jumped into the cart and started driving it fast. Bhim and his brothers were surprised and feared that he was trying to kidnap them. They were, after all, dressed in their best and wearing gold ornaments! All four boys started crying at the top of their voices.

After some time, the cart driver pointed to a light far ahead. 'That is the toll collector's booth. We will stop there for the night. Now stop crying.'

It was almost midnight when they reached the toll station. It was a little hut at the foot of a small hillock. They found many bullock carts parked there for the night. Bhim was relieved to see other people.

He asked the cart driver, 'Can we get water here? We are hungry and thirsty.'

'Go ask the toll booth operator. But don't tell him you are Mahars. Try saying you are Muslims instead.'

Bhim decided to follow his advice. He was confident he could speak like a Muslim. He was learning Urdu at school because Mahars were not allowed to learn Sanskrit, the language of the holy Hindu books.

Sadly, the toll booth manager told him rudely, 'Do you think we keep water for you Muslims here? Go to the village on top of the hill if you want water.'

In the dark, the hill looked scary to the tired boys. They reluctantly lay down in the unharnessed bullock cart and prepared for a sleepless night.

Morning arrived after a long wait. Onward they went in the bullock cart, hungry and thirsty. After a few hours' ride, they arrived at their father's doorstep, tired and shaken.

A surprised Ramji rushed out to receive them. That's when they learned that Ramji's assistant had forgotten to show him the letter from Bhim's brother!

The boys ran into their father's arms. They told him about their difficult emotional experience. Ramji didn't say much, just hugged them.

That journey to Koregaon left a deep impression on Bhim. He was aware they were untouchable. But the night he and his brothers had to go hungry and thirsty made him think long and hard about untouchability.

One day he asked his father, 'Baba, will we always remain untouchables and be treated so badly . . .?'

Ramji replied, 'No, son, we will have to change things, and we can.'

Bhim decided that's what he would do when he grew up. He studied hard and went to college in Bombay. Since he excelled in his studies, the Maharaja of Baroda gave him a scholarship to attend Columbia University in America.

When he returned to India, he taught economics and became a well-known scholar.

All the time he didn't forget his childhood resolution. He organized the untouchables to demand equal rights. He became a strong leader, an inspiring writer and an impressive speaker. While Bhim fought to end British rule in India, he also demanded protection and dignity for the untouchables.

He published a newspaper, *Bahishkrit Bharat* – meaning excluded India – to spread awareness about the discrimination they faced. He spent all his money on these activities even though this sometimes meant his family did not have enough. Being denied water had left a lasting impression on him. Years later, Bhim organized a peaceful

march of thousands of untouchables to drink water from a public pond as they were not allowed to use these. This historical event is famous as the Mahad Satyagraha.

Young Bhim became the tallest leader of the untouchables. He guided the making of the constitution of free India, which abolished untouchability and gave equal rights to all Indian citizens.

Throughout his life, he fought against injustice and inequality. Bhim wanted to free the untouchables from the unjust caste system. But he felt that the change was happening too slowly. Therefore, in 1956, along with thousands of his followers, he converted to Buddhism, a religion which has no caste system. He died a few months later.

His life and work brought about a historical change for the untouchables, who had suffered for centuries without rights and dignity. He continues to be an inspiration for people fighting for equal rights all over the world.

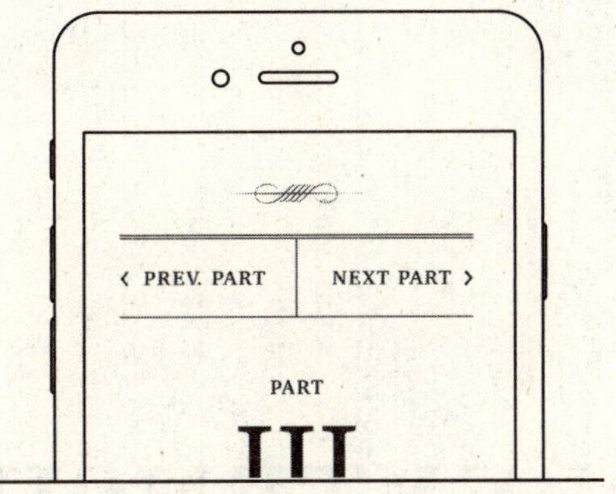


## Beautiful Typography

The quality of print transferred to your mobile. Forget ugly PDFs.

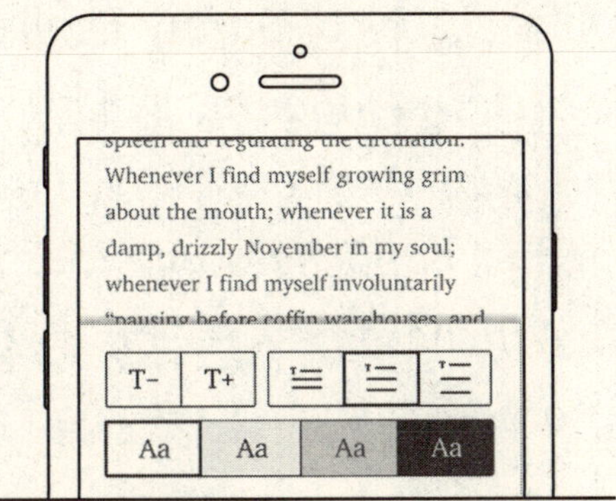


## Customizable Reading

Read in the font size, spacing and background of your liking.

# AN EXTENSIVE LIBRARY

*Including fresh, new, original Juggernaut books from the likes of Sunny Leone, Praveen Swami, Husain Haqqani, Umera Ahmed, Rujuta Diwekar and lots more. Plus, books from partner publishers and loads of free classics. Whichever genre you like, there's a book waiting for you.*

CRUCIBLES OF SIN
HITESHA
Can a Geek ever find Love?
Finding Juliet
Toffee
Mary Shelley
Frankenstein
A FAROOQ RESHI INVESTIGATION
COLD FLAKE
PRAVEEN SWAMI
A Psychiatrist's Guide To Heartbreak
How to Heal Your Broken Heart
DR SHYAM BHAT
MOIN and THE MONSTER
Mafia Queens of Mumbai
stories of women from the ganglands
S. Hussain Zaidi
with Jane Borges
Foreword by Vishal Bharadwaj
Pakistan's Queen of Romance
UMERA AHMED
Nowhere Girl
A Story of Love & Forgiveness
THE BEHEADING
This Is How He Will Bless Her
ABHEEK BARUA
THE Peshwa
The Lion and the Stallion
THE INVISIBLE WOMAN
SAURBH KATYAL
ANGRY BIRDS FAN? READ THE BOOK!
ANGRY BIRDS TOONS
TOONS TALES
ARCHANA SABOO
ADIKOOL
in
#AfricanAdventures
i am not a bimbette
Tarana Khan
She hates me. He loves me not but . . .
DON'T FALL IN LOVE
Vandana Shankar
KHUSHWANT SINGH
WE INDIANS

# DON'T JUST READ; INTERACT

*We're changing the reading experience from passive to active.*

## Ask authors questions

Get all your answers from the horse's mouth. Juggernaut authors actually reply to every question they can.

## Rate and review

Let everyone know of your favourite reads or critique the finer points of a book – you will be heard in a community of like-minded readers.

## Gift books to friends

For a book-lover, there's no nicer gift than a book personally picked. You can even do it anonymously if you like.

## Enjoy new book formats

Discover serials released in parts over time, picture books including comics, and story-bundles at discounted rates. And coming soon, audiobooks.

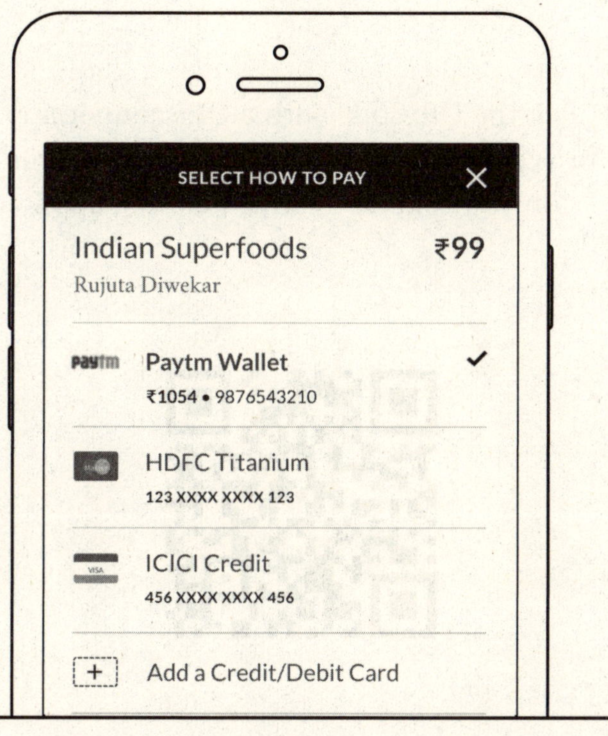


# Paytm Wallet, Cards & Apple Payments

On Android, just add a Paytm Wallet once and buy any book with one tap. On iOS, pay with one tap with your iTunes-linked debit/credit card.

Click the QR Code with a QR scanner app or type the link into the Internet browser on your phone to download the app.